ALAN HARRIS

Alan Harris's other plays include *For All I Care* (National Theatre of Wales); *Sugar Baby* (Dirty Protest); *How My Light Is Spent* (Royal Exchange Theatre, Manchester/Sherman Theatre/Theatre by the Lake; Bruntwood Judges' Prize 2015); *Love, Lies and Taxidermy* (Paines Plough/Sherman Theatre/Theatr Clwyd); *The Opportunity of Efficiency* (New National Theatre Tokyo/National Theatre Wales); *The Magic Toyshop* (Invisible Ink/Theatr Iolo); *The Future for Beginners* (liveartshow/Wales Millennium Centre); *A Good Night Out in the Valleys* (National Theatre Wales); *A Scythe of Time* (New York Musical Theatre Festival); *Cardboard Dad* (Sherman); *Orange* (Sgript Cymru). He has also written radio plays for BBC Radio 4 and Radio 3.

Libretti include *Marsha: A Girl Who Does Bad Things* (liveartshow/Arcola Grimeborn Festival); *The Hidden Valley* (Birdsong Opera/Welsh National Opera/Tête à Tête); *The Journey* (Welsh National Opera); *Rhinegold, Manga Sister* (both liveartshow/The Yard, London).

Other Titles in this Series

Alan Harris

FOR THE GRACE OF YOU GO I

NICK HERN BOOKS
London
www.nickhernbooks.co.uk

A Nick Hern Book

For The Grace Of You Go I first published in Great Britain in 2021 as a paperback original by Nick Hern Books Limited, The Glasshouse, 49a Goldhawk Road, London W12 8QP

For The Grace Of You Go I copyright © 2021 Alan Harris

Alan Harris has asserted his moral right to be identified as the author of this work

Extracts from the screenplay for *I Hired a Contract Killer* by Aki Kaurismäki are reproduced by permission of Sputnik Oy

Cover image: Dreamfly

Designed and typeset by Nick Hern Books, London
Printed in the UK by Mimeo Ltd, Huntingdon, Cambridgeshire PE29 6XX

A CIP catalogue record for this book is available from the British Library

ISBN 978 1 84842 966 6

For The Grace Of You Go I was commissioned by Theatr Clwyd and first performed at the Emlyn Williams Theatre, Theatr Clwyd, Mold, on 12 June 2021. The cast was as follows:

IRINA	Remy Beasley
MARK	Darren Jeffries
JIM	Rhodri Meilir

Director	James Grieve
Designer	Jacob Hughes
Lighting Designer	Katherine Williams
Sound Designer	Dominic Kennedy
Video Designer	Daniel Denton
Theatr Clwyd Carne	
Trainee Director	Francesca Goodridge

Producer	Ric Watts
Production Manager	Jim Davis
Company Stage Manager	Harriet Stewart
Deputy Stage Manager	Anna Hunscott
Wigs, Hair and	
Make-up Supervisor	Liz Armstrong (Wigs Up North)
Video Capture	Crayg Ward

For Theatr Clwyd	
Artistic Director	Tamara Harvey
Executive Director	Liam Evans-Ford

With thanks to all the team at Theatr Clwyd, Llyr Evans and Huws Gray (Flint).

It is work that sometimes stresses us out, and work that causes anxiety; but it is also work that can absorb us and take us out of ourselves until the clouds have gone. If work is the cause, it is also part of the cure. It was with work that Churchill pitchforked off his depression. And what was true for Churchill is basically true for all of us: that to a very large extent we derive our self-esteem from what we do. It is often from our jobs that we get that all-important sense of satisfaction. We can chase away those Black Dogs, boost the economy and save money, all at once.

Prime Minister B. Johnson

Characters

JIM
IRINA
MARK

Notes on Text

/ indicates a slight pause (these can add up)

– near or at the end of a line indicates an interruption

This text went to press before the end of rehearsals and so may differ slightly from the play as performed.

Jim

JIM AS DIRECTOR. Okay, okay, this is the set. I know – it
doesn't look like much but don't worry we'll green-screen
everything in later on. We've got the basics and all the
special-effects wizardry can happen later. I know. Fantastic.
No, no, it's actually cheaper than building everything. We're
shooting this in a linear timeline – think something like
Tangerine, you see that? No? Okay. We've got the three
cameras, so feel free to move around the space – I know
we've rehearsed but don't be afraid to follow your instincts if
something feels 'right', know what I mean? Okay. You all
set? Everyone on set all set? Jim – I'm going to give you very
little direction, you just do what you do. Great, Jim, maybe
take that as a starting position. Maybe a bit further left.
Perfecto. And maybe put your hands in your pockets? No.
You're right – why is the actor always right? – hands out of
pockets. Oh and I keep the camera rolling after the dialogue
has ended, so you just keep doing what you're doing, yeah?
It's a director thing. All set on set? Standby. Action.

Irina / Jim

That was. That was, I must admit. I was surprised.

/

Jim?

/

Give me something. You okay?

/

That was. Jim?

/

I couldn't believe the questions in there. Thanks for allowing me to sit in, to witness. She was, she had no idea you were uncomfortable. And the room-divide thing – we could hear, could you hear everything that poor woman was saying next door? Then the sobbing, we could actually hear her sobbing. That's not right. You know, when you went to the loo, I asked about the, and the assessor said it's not usually like this but they divided the room because there's a shortage of computer screens – does that even make sense? How you feeling Jim?

/

Asking. Do you wash yourself in the morning and then when I said 'of course he washes himself in the morning' she actually tut-tutted. Did you hear her tut? You do wash yourself in the mornings, Jim? Course you do. Can you walk to the front door? Do you use public transport? Do you have any pets? I asked the assessor, after, about the washing-machine question – can *you* use one, how! – and she said if it's 'in the affirmative' it means you can handle modern technology. I felt like telling her...

/

You okay, Jim?

/

They're all trick questions.

What?

If you say yes, then they don't give you any points.

But you answered yes to all those questions.

Except the pets one.

/

They don't understand you can have issues while still being able to put a quick wash on.

/

Sorry, who are you again?

Irina. I told you. Before. Yes?

/

My company – well, not my company, it's Mr Mazio's
company, has been asked to be part of a pilot, a new scheme to
get people back into work.

Sorry?

And the best way to identify people – quickly, *sans* red tape –
is to sit in on PIP interviews.

The government pays your company to get people off benefits?

There is a financial incentive but that's not why we're doing it,
why I'm doing it.

Sorry, I'm a lost cause.

No! Look, you answered all their questions 'in the affirmative'
– let's take that to its conclusion – why not do something else?

What?

Be part of our scheme. Work can set you free, Jim.

You know who said that?

Boris Johnson?

Close.

Look, it's a government pilot scheme, helping people with
'issues' back into work –

Is this some kind of Remploy...? I'm not –

No, no, these are real jobs. Someone from the DWP asked us to
– I'm a manager at a terrific company – find suitable
candidates.

What's it called, this scheme?

'Work Hard and Make Something of Yourself.'

Really?

No. Jokes.

/

Doesn't have a name. Yet. Building a country that works for everyone starts here, Jim.

With me?

Fantastic. I'll get the ball rolling.

Really – as easy as that?

I'm a manager. I can do these things. What do you say? I have the feeling you are going to be a terrific worker, Jim.

Jim

JIM *is on the production line – he's quick and good at his job.*

Along with the pizzas that come along the line, there's a rosette that JIM *picks up and pins on himself. It says 'Employee of the Month'.*

What? Me?

(*Then a trophy.*

He's having a wonderful time. But then:)

Irina / Jim

Again.

JIM *quickly drops the rosette and trophy back onto the line –* IRINA *is not aware of them.*

Again.

/

Again.

/

Again. Come on, Jim, you're getting slower, not faster.

Sorry, Irina, I can get faster but with you watching me it's difficult. It's, like, more pressure than normal. Not that pressure is bad, I thrive on pressure. Pressure is my middle name. Jim 'Pressure' Leach, that's –

Okay, okay. I'll stop the production line, yeah, for a minute. Jim, this is a job that requires speed and accuracy. Eight per ten secs is min.

I know. I know it's all about speed and accuracy.

And your speed is just not... speedy enough. Jim, the Mazio Pattern was designed personally by Mr Mazio so every pizza looks individual. It's very important to the company identity. You know we can't call these handmade pizzas without your very vital input –

Putting the meat on top?

We could get a machine to do it – but machines don't have hands, do they?

I realise that.

So if machines did it we couldn't put 'handmade' on the box.

And two quid on the price.

Exactly. Consumers aspire to better things, Jim. They want bespoke meal plans, custom-fit clothing, made-to-measure kitchens and handmade pizzas – and those hands are yours, Jim. I don't think you appreciate the responsibility you have here.

Putting pepperoni on pizzas?

You are a vital cog in the raising of standards in this country.

When you said 'work', I imagined... but I can get faster.

The required level of pizza production is to place six pieces of meat on eight pizzas per ten seconds in this section. Agreed?

I can get to eight. Beyond that. Ten. Easy. I'll show you – start the line back up. I'm ready.

You're not the only one under pressure here, Jim.

/

I've gone out on a limb for you, Jim.

Won't let you down.

Mr Mazio has told me to tell people that you, people like you, have to have the same standards as the rest of the employees. I wasn't completely aware of that when I offered you the –

But doesn't the government pay my wages?

That's a naive way of looking at it.

/

/

Look, if you fail, I fail. And I can't afford to fail. I moved here. We've bought an apartment, this is a long-term thing for me.

Just give me a proper chance. Please, Irina.

You're capable of getting up to eight?

I'm up to four.

Four is nowhere near eight.

Do you know in some cultures four is considered the same as eight?

/

Is this going to be an issue, Jim?

Film / Jim

JIM AS DIRECTOR. Okay, Jim, this next scene is what we call
a transition. It lets the audience know where our hero is.
Where are you? Finished work, knackered, going to the pub.
But the modern-day cinema-goer doesn't just want to know
where you are physically – they want to know where you are
mentally. Yes, through action you have to convey every
nuance of your character. While walking into a pub. Can you
do that? Give it a try. All set on set? And... Action!

(JIM *walks into a pub*.)

Cut! Try it again, Jim – remember, nuance. And... Action.

(JIM *walks into a pub*.)

Mark / Jim

Do we get tea and biscuits afterwards?

No.

Right.

/

/

Do people go and have a drink, together?

No.

/

Not that I drink.

/

Mark.

Jim.

/

/

Do you do conversation, Jim?

Do you know any plumbers?

Sorry?

We've had a quote to fix our boiler. Not cheap, boilers. I'm saving up, a bit every week. But if I can get the quote down it means –

New in town. Ish.

/

Bought. Luxury development. Corunna Court.

/

The old barracks site?

/

Got a sweet spot – only place with a double garage and a south-facing Juliet balcony. I can see the A5152 from my living room.

What's a Juliet balcony?

It's like a balcony but smaller.

/

/

I read – in *Men's Health* – that hot showers are a real boost for a person's well-being. If I can just get a hot shower every day then –

You take *Men's Health*?

No. It's in the post office. I read the magazines while I'm in the queue. They're not keen on that.

/

And it's important to keep things clean, isn't it? You can only do that with hot water.

/

So how does this work?

This is just the film night. Sometimes we then get together and discuss stuff, topics the film might have brought up for us, how we feel. Then, next time, someone else chooses a film.

Who's chosen this one?

Anne.

She looks a bit arty, Jim.

/

Subtitles, Jim?

Possibly.

Oh God.

/

/

How did you wind up here?

My significant other told me about it (always trying to 'improve me') and I thought, what the heck, I like movies...

/

Why is it we're shy of who we are, Jim?

Sorry?

Even this night is like, it's under the carpet, isn't it? No posters up for 'loony movie night'. You ever been to the States?

/

The United States of God Bless America?

No. Not travelled.

No vacations with your partner?

Sorry?

You said 'we'. 'Our' boiler.

Figure of speech.

Oh.

/

/

They all have therapists. In the States. Seriously. And they talk about them all the time. My therapist said this, my therapist told me that – it's like more than normal over there.

They do seem different. The Americans I've met. Or seen.

I should have been American.

You still can be – pretend to be one. Wear a big hat. Or just go there.

No can do.

/

Won't let me back in. You drive, Jim?

Never passed my test.

But you've heard of road rage, right? I had a problem with road rage while Stateside. An incident with a Buick driver in Ohio.

Was it your fault?

Definitely.

/

/

Shouldn't be long. I think Anne's just gone in to sort the projector thing out.

/

What do you, uh, do, Mark?

Words are my tools.

Sorry?

Writer. Online.

Oh, very, must be interesting.

Can be. I write for military magazines.

There's magazines for the military?

Loads.

I take it you were in the army?

Yes, sir.

Right.

You ever serve?

No.

/

Did you enjoy it?

All I'd ever wanted to do.

But did you enjoy it?

It was different to what I was expecting.

/

/

And you? Do you do something?

I'm in artisan food production.

Wow. *You* own a business?

No, no. Mr Mazio owns the business. I'm... below Mr Mazio. You heard of Mazio's?

I have.

It's a terrific place to work. Haven't been there that long, but... every month, if someone hits a certain target, they (plus a guest) fly out for a weekend to Mr Mazio's villa in Rome.

And you're in line for this?

Nothing's certain, Mark, but, you know – like Mum always used to say, 'Why can't it be me?'

Why not indeed?

I'm on a brilliant project – you work for the company, sort of still on benefits but you get wages.

Right.

It's part of the government's push to help those with mental health get back into work.

I've heard the speeches. What's it called? This scheme?

Not sure it's got a name.

They've always got a name – helps with the PR.

If there is a name I've not been told it.

/

Who you gonna take to Rome, is there…?

Sorry?

To Roma?

Uh, not sure.

/

There are certain pressures, though. At Mazio's.

Boss busting your balls?

My manager…

Go on, spill the beans – a real asshole, huh?

Everyone could do with chilling out a bit, you know. I don't know if I'm coming or going and this supervisor is standing there with a stopwatch. A stopwatch.

Bummer.

/

Bet you hate it when you tell her something – something logical – and she just goes right ahead and ignores it, huh? Bet that really pisses you off.

Never said it was a 'she'.

Sorry – Weinstein. Shoot me. Gender stereotyping. Shoot me.

/

And I bet her focus is all over the place – when she should be helping you, she's helping some other schmuck. Isn't that the case? It's so typical...

Schmuck, *busting your balls*, *spill the beans*, *asshole*. You sound a bit American, Mark.

Thank you.

/

Kids, Jim?

No.

Pets?

I don't even have much furniture.

I get it – La-Z-Boy and a widescreen –

No –

No TV?

/

For real? Jesus Christ, Jim, what is life to you?

Actually, Mark, at this point, I'm not entirely sure but –

Things are going well?

How can you tell?

/

/

So, what's the movie?

It's from Finland.

They make movies in Finland?

One was even nominated for an Oscar in 2002 – *The Man Without a Past*. Now that's a great film.

What was last month's?

Joulukuusivarkaat.

Finnish?

/

Have these people never heard of Bruce Willis?

/

How many Finnish movies have you seen, Jim?

Seventeen. I've also seen twenty-three Japanese films and nineteen from Nigeria.

Jeez – you've been coming here too long.

/

/

It'll be subtitled.

Suppose.

What's tonight's called? Probably hasn't got an English title even, I bet.

Oh, it has.

/

It's called: *I Hired a Contract Killer*.

/

/

I think it's about to start, Mark.

/

(*The film starts* – I Hired a Contract Killer.)

Film

We see the start of I Hired a Contract Killer *by Aki Kaurismäki.*

*The opening credits – the first shot of Henri at his desk –
canteen scene with Henri sitting on his own.*

Irina / Jim

JIM, *still lost in the film, is missing pizzas going through the
production line. He's struggling to keep up.*

Speed isn't the only thing.

Sorry? What?

Mr Mazio, unfortunately, has been alerted to your, uh, accuracy.
You've gone against the pattern.

So would you.

No, I wouldn't. I was hasty giving you this job –

Stuck in this white room, ten hours a day. It's fucking shit, Irina.
I can't stand it. Could you do this for ten hours a day? Couldn't
I even have the radio on? If you worked here, right in this spot –

I wouldn't start arranging the pepperoni into 'words' and
'images' on Mr Mazio's pizzas.

You might.

How would you feel if you got a pizza that had the pepperoni in the shape of a word?

I might find it intriguing.

Mr Mazio does not find it intriguing to open up his Twitter feed and find complaints.

You don't know what it's like to stand here for ten hours a –

A tweet from @amy_falk: why does my Mazio pizza have a picture of a sad smiley face? A tweet from @eric_thered: just opened up a Mazio pizza and I'm sure the pepperoni is in the shape of a unicorn #lotsofmeat

Have I told you that sometimes I think my arms are not part of me – they have a mind of their own?

I can't help you with that.

I stopped doing the pictures.

But you continued to spell out words on over six hundred pizzas, didn't you?

/

Mr Mazio is disappointed.

So am I. I'm a disappointment to me. But I can fix this, Irina, let me fix this. I need to fix this. There's no heating in my house – has your boiler ever broken down? You ever shower in cold water? You do it enough times, it does something to your soul.

I don't think you realise… this is the real world, Jim… it's not just you that has targets. Don't you think I've got targets? I've got targets coming out of my ears. Out of my… eyes. And if I don't make those targets… You know, there's this six-month thing. And that's coming up. Probation. It's not called probation but that's what it is. Mr Mazio calls it the 'bedding-in period' but that's what it says in my contract and it's not just you who hasn't been, what, performing, but you are the worst, the others are just slow or whatever and you know how that makes me feel?

Okay, okay, calm –

I have to release you.

What?

Sorry, you're not making the grade – I have no choice.

Release? You mean sack? You can't sack me, I'm on a
government scheme –

Release –

Me? No.

Speed and accuracy.

No, no.

You fail on one, maybe we can fix. You fail on two and people
notice.

What people?

First the customers – let's not forget they're the most important.

The audience don't mind.

Audience?

I mean customers.

And then Mr Mazio knows and when Mr Mazio knows (he's
very aware of the company's reputation, he responds to any
negative comment on Twitter within four minutes), then I know,
believe me he lets me know in no uncertain terms. Mr Mazio is
not an easy man to deal with, you're lucky you don't have to –
and I have to do something about it.

You can't sack –

Release –

Me. I need this job. You told me anyone can be a success if they
work hard enough.

After he said we're going to be part of this scheme, my belief in
productivity – of people and places – marked me out, you'll be
perfect to head up our 'Work Hard and Make Something of
Yourself' Scheme which, to be fair, I thought I'd be running in

Cardiff, not Wrexham, and he says it fits in with our handmade-we-care-about-the-community the we're-not-Domino's-big-corporate-pizzas thing we have going on – he tweeted about it.

And is Mr Mazio going to tweet that you've sacked me?

/

I'll take a pay cut. I don't need much. I've started to trim my own hair. I do my own dental work. I bought a kit from the internet – I've done two of my own fillings. Look, see, at the back.

Shouldn't your landlord sort that out?

My teeth?

The boiler.

He should. He really should. But he's not.

Complain.

To who? The landlord?

I have to be a success here, Jim. At night I dream about this line, this very line and it's going fast and then it's going slower and slower and as it goes slower my heart goes slower until it's almost at a stop and if I can't make it go faster then... we've bought a bloody apartment, not just rented, Mark said we should rent first but I was like no, let's jump straight in and now, now, now, now, now, now

Okay, sit. Here, sit, breathe. In and out, in and out. Keep breathing. Yeah, that's it, keep breathing, steady breaths. In and out, Irina.

/

/

Oh God, I'm sorry.

No, no, it's fine. You've nothing to be sorry about. Except wanting to sack me. Keep breathing.

The line's not moving! The line should be moving! –

No, look, take a second, you've just had some kind of –

I'm fine.

You're not.

Thank you. Thank you for helping me through that.

I can make eight, Irina.

Jim –

I can. And I'll stop writing words on the pizzas.

If our numbers are down any more, Mr Mazio, if he gets any more tweets –

He won't get any more tweets, I promise. And my numbers – eight. If not more. I'm going to be your best employee.

/

When you said I'd be working for an artisan food producer I thought it was going to be different this time.

What did you imagine?

/

I –

Yes?

/

This was a fresh start – a chance to show that the problem isn't me.

I'm not sure I can help you –

You can't release me now. I just saved your life.

Not sure that's true –

We're both under pressure, I can see that now – it's going to spur me on, yeah? All I needed was an incentive.

/

You won't tell anyone about this? Me, having this –

Who'm I going to tell?

Thank you.

Think nothing of it, Irina. Let's go.

Let's go?

I can do it.

You can do it. Okay, yeah, right. Let's... I'll start up the line. Ready?

My arms are part of me. There is no little man in my brain.

That's good. And... go.

/

/

/

Again.

Film / Jim

I Hired a Contract Killer. *In the film, Henri is alone in his flat, drinking a cup of tea, eating a scone and listening to the radio.*

Cross-fade to JIM, *in exactly the same position in his flat, also alone, doing exactly the same thing.*

Mark / Irina

They're at the back of the cupboard, can you reach?

Getting these people back to work is spot on in theory... but in reality –

Okay, I'll get them.

I mean, just cos you've had some kind of mental whatever-it-is in the past doesn't mean you can't stick bits of meat on a pizza, does it?

June 2020. Do pine nuts go off? Wasabi, wasabi, wasabi…

/

Remember the first time you had wasabi? That sushi joint in Paris?

You told me it was pureed peas.

Whole mouthful. Classic. You actually started to cry.

Got us a free meal, though, didn't it?

That waiter – I couldn't believe it when you told him you were crying cos you missed your dog so much.

The French love dogs.

/

What are you doing?

What?

I just saw you. You just ate –

It's nothing. These nuts will be fine.

What did you just take?

Xanax.

What?

It's nothing – helps me relax.

But –

You want one?

You can't –

They're not even a real drug.

They are.

Relax.

But –

My therapist recommends them.

You're –

Every now and again, as a supplement.

I didn't know you'd started with a therapist in – Wrexham.

She's terrific.

And she's prescribed these?

As a supplement.

To your usual medication?

It's what she said so… relax. What about this guy, come on, tell me.

It's as if the guy, this guy, wants to fail.

You shouldn't do it.

What?

Let Mazio make you shoulder the responsibility for this scheme. It's just guilt.

Sorry?

You haven't got time to spend with me so you fill more of your time helping other people.

We talk, Mark. When don't we – talk?

Kidding. You do your job, I'm fine.

Really?

Pine nuts. They last forever, right?

Look, Mark, forget that, is there something on your – mind?

You know you shouldn't hire people just cos –

What?

You hired him because of me, didn't you?

It's a government scheme –

Come on. I'm not stupid. You went on some crusade – a very
Irina crusade – to hire people with a mental-health history
because of me. Because of me –

No, no, when I was transferred, Mr Mazio said this was my
role, he told me and I thought, yeah, I believe in getting people
back into – work

You mean this wasn't a choice? *Transferred?* You made it sound
like a choice to come and work up here –

He made it sound like a choice but looking back –

Thanks, Irina.

/

I'm worried about you –

Perfectly fine –

/

I believe in giving people, things, places, chances, yes? Is that a
crime?

/

But you want to sack him? Thought it was like a guaranteed
spot.

/

I don't 'want' to but… Mr Mazio is insistent. We can sack them
if it's performance-related.

Sounds –

What?

Is that the sort of company you want to work for, Irina?

It's… work, Mark.

It's just typical of you – you hire the guy and then you're firing
his ass. Does this taste a bit bitter? I think these nuts are off.

Working is just… obviously not working for him.

Maybe this is the best version of this man that can be. At this particular point in his life. Come on, relax. Let's talk about something that's not work. Yeah?

/

/

Yeah, I'm, it's just. I got to say I'm under a bit of pressure. And this guy is… I want to help him but –

You fancy him?

Oh come on, Mark – why d'you have to turn everything, I'm worried that Mr Mazio is going to fire *me* –

What part of work are we not talking about?

You don't really think I fancy him, do you?

/

/

How was the film-club thing? Good?

Oh talking about me now, are we?

Oh come on.

It was kinda lame.

What was the film?

I Hired a Contract Killer.

Really? At a mental-health film night?

The ending really got me pissed. Our hero has nothing to live for, takes out the contract on himself, falls in love and is about to get rubbed out when the assassin, can you believe this, is the one who dies. He's suffering from terminal cancer and shoots himself!

Sounds different. Thank you for this, I appreciate it, boy, these are tense, we got to get these loose –

Let's leave.

Sorry?

I hate this town.

We've only been here a few months.

That's enough. Let's leave.

Give it a chance – you're hardly here anyway, some conference or thing every other weekend, you're always at –

Let's go back to Cardiff. You're not happy, I'm not happy. Let's leave. It's the logical conclusion. Yes? Decision made, yes?

We always knew the first few months would be tough.

Don't ignore my logical conclusions, Irina.

You know I've always had a passion for food –

It's a pizza factory –

That I want to make my career in food. You encouraged me to take this transfer.

When I thought it was a choice!

/

Okay – hands up. I was wrong. Happy now?

We've hardly explored –

I've explored.

But not together.

Believe me – Wrexham doesn't get any better the more you 'explore'. In fact, it gets worse.

We've bought this place, Mark.

Then let's sell it.

Easy as that?

Rent it out then. Let's move back to Cardiff.

I'm doing –

You can do that anywhere.

We can build a future here, Mark, finally put down some roots.

Without that job I think we have the opportunity to experience life.

/

This is our chance to shine, Irina.

We can do that here.

There is nothing to do here.

There is.

Like what?

I don't know – I haven't explored yet. I can't fail, Mark.

Why not?

I've worked hard – I'm supposed to succeed.

/

/

What's wrong with him? This fella at work.

Some sort of disorder – depersonalisation? – which you'd think would be a bonus for someone repeatedly laying out a pattern of cold meats on a pizza base.

Why have we never been to Rome?

What?

Is it true that Mazio's gives out free trips to Rome? Surely if anyone is getting free trips to –

No one goes to Rome.

What?

How do you know about Rome...?

You mentioned it – when you started.

Oh, well, no one goes. A carrot that is forever out of reach – no one ever reaches the targets.

Surely the staff must realise that –

They never see each other. It's in sections. Dough never sees tomato never sees pepperoni. They all think someone else is going to Rome.

Pretty fucking shitty.

It's an excellent motivational tool that –

But it's not the truth.

/

/

Just let me get things, let's get my six-months review over with and then things will get better.

There's only so much hanging around Eagles Meadow I can stand, Irina. You're not the only one under pressure.

But your articles are selling – you said you were selling articles to new websites every week. You said, you said you had a new commission for a piece for that *Military Software* magazine –

Military Hardware magazine. Not everything is about work, Irina.

/

/

This is ruined. I've got to bin this now. Ruined. Why didn't you tell me pine nuts go off? I might open a bottle of wine. Just a glass, before you say anything… have one with me.

Better not – got to get up early tomorrow.

Better not?

Come on, Mark.

I was in Starbucks today – yes Wrexham has a Starbucks – and I realised how much time I waste on doing nothing. Waiting. Thinking about waiting. Waiting for my name to be called for a latte, waiting for you to come home, waiting for the bus, the train –

You should get more Ubers –

Waiting for taxis, waiting for the micro to go round, waiting for the washing, waiting for, I'm a man who is waiting in a country that is very fond of waiting and things are building up, Irina.

Okay, okay. Don't get worked up. What can I do?

Leave with me. It's the logical conclusion.

/

/

I need to get this, it's Mr Mazio. We can talk about this, we should talk about this when I've finished on the phone.

Don't answer that.

Really? Let's have dinner out tomorrow night? I'll get off early.

I'm busy tomorrow night – don't answer the phone. Let's talk now.

/

Hello? Mr Mazio. *Buonasera*.

Film / Jim

In I Hired a Contract Kiler, *Henri enters the Honolulu Bar.*

On stage JIM *is copying Henri, playing out the film.*

He makes the same actions as Henri – but we, the audience, are the people in the bar.

He mouths Henri's words:

HENRI. A ginger ale.

Where I come from, we eat places like this for breakfast.

(But the next line in the film is a revelation to JIM. *He doesn't mouth it:)*

I need a killer.

Mark / Jim

That was some of the worst acting I've seen in ages.

/

The movie. The other night? Jim? Earth to Jim.

I know what you mean, Mark – but, also, it was kind of good at the same time.

You want a drink?

Ginger ale.

I might have a glass of wine. Just the one – even the thought of that movie has driven me to drink.

Ha!

You think they named this place The Bank cos it was a bank?

/

/

Would you ever...

Mark?

No, I can't even say it.

What?

It's goddamn silly if I say it out loud.

Goddamn say it, Mark.

Would you ever consider doing anything like that? Like the man in the film. Kill yourself.

Uh, right, let's jump straight into… he doesn't, he tries to but can't, so he hires someone else to do it.

Pretty cowardly, huh?

It might be harder to kill yourself than you imagine.

/

/

Cheers.

Cheers.

/

/

I suppose, in the army, you killed people. Sorry, you might not want to talk about –

No. Never got near… It's one of my many regrets.

That you didn't kill anyone?

I was in the army, Jim, it's what you're supposed to do.

/

/

What's it like to have DPD?

We don't have to talk about me.

Go on.

Let's talk about you.

I'm curious.

Um. The best image I can come up with is that, sometimes, there's a little man sat in the back of my head, with the controls,

and I can see the inside of my skull and I'm looking at the man
and he's looking out of these two eye sockets.

/

When I first spoke to someone about it, the words I used were:
'I've gone mad. It's finally happened, I've gone mad.'

/

Sometimes, Mark, I'm in this movie but I've got to build the set
and then I'm in a scene but also watching the scene. Like, I'm
watching me going down one of those ski runs they have, the
black run for professionals and skiing types?, and I'm racing
downhill and there's no stopping, but I know, at some point, I'm
going to crash. You ever get that feeling?

Whoooa. Floodgates. Open.

/

Sorry.

/

I suspect you don't have many friends, do you, Jim?

Not really.

Are you lonely, Jim?

Sometimes.

But you've got someone who you can talk about these feelings
with, Jim?

I'm talking to you about them.

I don't count. I'm not that interested.

There's Irina.

Yeah?

Yeah, it's a bit complicated – she's my boss but she seems to be
everyone's friend at work – not sure how she fits it all in –

Probably by ignoring her home life.

I can talk to her, you know – except when she's in work. It's like she's got a split personality.

Maybe she's the one who needs a therapist.

No –

And you can talk to your therapist?

/

Don't be ashamed of that, Jim.

I don't have a therapist.

You've every right to see a therapist, Jim.

Thank you. But I can't afford one. When I was on benefits I saw someone but that was just filling in a form and then I waited to actually speak to someone and no one got back to me so –

Maybe you can take her to Rome?

Who?

This Irina woman. Take her on a date, Nando's, and bam! – come to Rome with me.

No, no –

Why not?

We're not suitable. I'm a bit older than she is and I think she's in a relationship –

She could be older than she looks.

What if she's younger than she looks?

Older men can be attractive, Jim.

I know but –

Four syllables.

/

Michael Douglas.

No. Me? No. Uh. Do you have a therapist, Mark?

Don't really need one.

But –

I'm beyond that. In fact, I've started to experiment with coming off my medication.

Is that wise?

Time will tell. Have you ever tried these?

What are –

Xanax.

No, I tried antidepressants, SSRIs, but they weren't –

Go on, have one, I've got plenty.

/

Internet. From the States.

Thanks but I'm good with the ginger ale.

Your loss, buddy.

/

/

I've ordered a pizza.

What?

They do Mazio's pizzas here, can you believe that? I thought it was very American – to have a bar in Wrexham where you can have a brewski and an artisan pizza.

I'm off pizza.

No, of course, didn't think, you must be sick –

/

You lonely, Mark?

People might think being a writer is lonely but it's not – I've got editors at me all day, I go to conferences, I can't go to Eagles Meadow without seeing someone I know, I've stopped going to

Starbucks because they are like 'hey, Mark – latte?', it's like walking into an episode of *Cheers*, I have too many people in my life, I have the support of a wonderful, loving partner. How could I be lonely?

/

/

That's our number.

/

/

I got pepperoni. You sure you'll not want a… well, look at that.

Yeah.

It looks like. Looks like, the pepperoni is, is that a word?

More of a sentence.

Hell… trap.

It says: Help me, I'm trapped.

In pepperoni!

Yup.

I didn't know they were doing that. That's so cool. I'm going to take a picture and tweet about it.

No. Don't.

That is cool.

/

Unless someone *is* trapped.

/

Man, you sure you don't want a slice?

Positive.

/

/

It's an interesting concept, isn't it, Jim, and it's what we're doing all the time anyway?

What is?

The movie. *I Hired a Contract Killer.* We know we're going to die at some point. We could walk out that door and be hit by a car, 'he was hit by a car outside The Bank, stepped off the sidewalk', but to say I know I'm definitely going to walk out that door and at some point I'm definitely going to be hit by a car (or by some other means of death) is kind of liberating, no?

I'm not sure.

I liked that movie, in spite of the bad acting.

Anne's choices are always good – even if they tend to be subtitled.

This pizza is gooooooood. Drink up, Jim, I'll get you another ginger ale.

Film / Jim

JIM AS DIRECTOR. Okay, all set? Ready for your big Alpine scene, Jim? Rolling. Action!

(JIM *is in work. A snow globe comes along the production line.* JIM *picks it up and shakes it. An Alpine scene on the green screen.*

On the production line comes a woolly hat. JIM *puts it on. Gloves. The same. Two skiing poles.* JIM *takes them and jumps on the conveyor belt.*

JIM *realises he's going too fast and starts to scream, when:*)

Irina / Jim

What you doing?

Huh?

I'm stopping the line.

No, don't.

There. It's stopped. Because of you.

Start it up.

Pizzas are going through with no meat on them – these are pepperoni pizzas, Jim.

I was just…

You okay?

To work?

You looked as if you were away with the fairies –

I'm okay.

/

The pilot scheme has ended, Jim.

That's fine – things end, I know – I can work like the normal employees.

Should you be using the word 'normal'?

/

We have to start the production line back up now, Jim.

I just get a bit overwhelmed.

Don't cry.

I'm not.

Please, Jim.

/

/

Jim, believe me when I say this, I want to give you a hug but HR says we're not allowed to touch anyone. Can I give you a pretend hug?

/

Is that better?

Don't know what's wrong with me, Irina, I'm not a cryer.

/

Can you be honest with me, Irina?

Try my best.

Am I in the running for Rome?

I just told you the pilot scheme has come to an end.

/

/

I'm ready now. Let's go, Irina.

No.

What?

Sorry to say this, Jim, but we've got to release you. For sure, this time. But I'm not sacking you – the government is.

No, I'm doing my best.

I know but –

But if you sack me I'll have to...

Think of this as a learning experience.

I'll have to apply for PIP again, then that'll get turned down and then I have to appeal and see an assessor who will ask me stupid questions about pets and washing machines and ignore my needs and... Oh God. These walls are not even real, are they?

We have a queue of empty pizzas. Sorry, Jim, my hands are tied.

No, they're not. If they are, untie them.

Decisions have been made.

Is it because I took a break? I'll take my breaks in break time. Honest.

Listen to me, Jim. I'm going to tell you the real, very real reason I have to let you go: you are the worst employee we have.

Understand you're under pressure, Irina, from the powers that be. I can go quicker.

Even if you do go, what? Fifteen per cent quicker, you will still be the slowest employee we have. Mazio's could offer you a real job but you're not up to it.

Think I'm developing arthritis.

Then this is not the job for you.

But I need this job. Have you got a boiler?

You've failed, Jim.

Sorry?

To impress. To hold down this job. I wish there was something else I could say but you have to move away from this fucking line and make room for someone else who is going to do the job to a satisfactory standard and reflect well on me because we have, I have, bent over backwards, made every reasonable provision for your illness but at the end of the day you are fucking things up and I will not have things fucked up by you, so fuck off. Move away from the fucking pizzas.

I thought we were buddies?

/

I think this job is holding you back, Jim.

No, it's not, it's the only thing that's keeping me going.

Without this job I think you have the opportunity to experience life.

Are you crazy?

This is your chance to shine, Jim.

Life scares the shit out of me. I see life as a series of scenes that I have no control over.

You can change that.

/

/

You are crazy. You're doing this to me.

No.

Why can't you just let me work?

Because you're fucking up my ratings, because the line is fucking stopped, because you're affecting profits.

It's down to you. If you said it was okay for me to continue –

If you want someone to blame –

I can't blame the government. I can't blame Mazio. I can't see Mazio so I can't blame him. Bring him here and I'll blame him, you're the one I can see, Irina.

Film / Jim

On screen we see a scene from I Hired a Contract Killer *in which Henri is sacked:*

BOSS. I'm sure you'll understand we have to begin with foreigners.

HENRI. I understand. When do I have to go?

BOSS. As your position here, for some reason, has never been official, two weeks' notice is out of the question.

HENRI. Right away?

BOSS. Yes, if you please.

(*Then, on stage:*)

JIM AS MR MAZIO. We're making changes here at Mazio's –
I'm sure you'll understand we have to start with people like
you, Jim.

JIM. I understand. When do I have to go?

Mark / Jim

Drink?

Uh, no, really, that's not really, thanks for seeing me, Mark. I've
got no one else to talk – to

We have a fine selection of drinks, sir. We should open a bottle
of wine.

Mark, I want to ask you something.

Sit. Relax. Why the rush? Let's have some polite conversation.

But I have something I want to –

Come on buddy, relax.

/

/

It's a nice apartment. Not much of a view though – is that the
A5152?

I like seeing the freeway. Reminds me of the States.

Mum always said to me, 'Jim, the world is a book, all you have
to do to turn the pages is travel.'

Amen to that.

But she never left Wrexham.

/

/

I stopped working months ago.

Mark?

My wife thinks I'm still writing. I haven't sold anything in months… I don't see the point.

/

Don't you think –

I hang around. I wait. I drink coffee in Starbucks. She's too busy to see that it's only her contributing to the joint account.

Why, Mark?

Why, what?

Why do you feel you have to hide this from your wife?

No one's telling the truth, so why should I?

But you're being truthful to me?

Always, Jim.

/

I'm going to take a hot shower.

Uh, now? Mark?

Wash off the dirt from the day.

Uh /

Wait right there, young man. I'll be two ticks.

Uh, right but I need to ask you something… Mark? Mark?

/

/

Order a pizza.

Um, no.

Irina

IRINA *sits alone, she has a Mazio's for lunch. She opens the box. The pizza has a message on it. It says:*

'If not now, when?'

Mark / Jim

You want me to do it? Order the pizza? You're shy.

No, I. Mark?

Yes?

This is a bit unnerving now, you standing there in a dressing gown and me standing here.

Weird is the new normal.

/

Sit here.

I'm fine where I am.

Come on, there's plenty of room here.

/

/

Do you want to have sex with me, Mark?

Isn't that why you're here?

Where did you get that from?

I just feel you've... chosen me.

I have but –

I have sex with a stranger every other weekend.

/

My wife thinks I'm at magazine conferences. If she knew how much I spend each month on Booking.com she'd hit the roof.

Sorry, I –

Come on, Jim, we're here for the same thing.

We're not.

Is this some sort of game? If this is your idea of foreplay then it's not –

No. Please. Let go of my wrist.

Ha! Look at your face. I'm kidding, Jim! *I just feel you've... chosen me.* Peachy. You're too easy to punk. Look at your face. It was a joke, Jim. I don't really have sex with strangers.

Do you really fancy me?

Relax, buddy, I was just fooling.

I want you to kill me.

/

/

Sorry?

Simple as. Like in the film.

The film?

The man in the film.

You want me to...

You were in the army.

You really want me to... like the man in the movie?

Like him. Though I'm not like him. I'm not going to meet someone, fall in love and change my mind.

You know what would happen now, don't you?

What?

If this was a movie –

This is –

Or we were in America, you'd meet someone, fall in love and change your mind.

There's shit-all chance of that happening. We're in Wrexham.

You're serious?

I am.

/

/

I can't do it myself, Mark. Believe me, I've tried. Before. And suicide doesn't make a great movie.

/

/

Okay.

You're not going to talk me out of it?

Do you want me to?

No.

Okay.

/

/

So, you'll do it?

It's… big.

I realise that.

We hardly know each other.

That's best, yes? Like *Strangers on a Train*.

/

What's in it for me?

You said you regretted not –

I know, but, you know, I regret not taking up the piano but I'm still not going to lessons.

/

Mark?

I do this sometimes – put barriers in the way of what I really want. It's the 'because' syndrome, I'd like to do this but I can't because, I'd like to do that but I can't because. It's bullshit.

You want to do this?

I think I might want to do this.

/

You really want me to do this?

Yes.

/

So, you'll do it?

/

/

/

Deal?

Deal.

/

/

Any idea how you'll...

How would you like to… Jim?

I'd rather it didn't hurt, I'm not so brave.

That's tricky.

Quick then. I mean quick.

Quick I can do.

/

/

Right, uh, from this point on I'll leave my front door unlocked.

You definitely want me to kill you?

Yes.

Film / Jim

JIM, *in his apartment, sits in a chair.*

On screen, Henri is in the Honolulu bar, talking to two gangsters.

GANGSTER 1. Why'd you want to die, Henri?

HENRI. For personal reasons.

GANGSTER 2. But life is beautiful.

GANGSTER 1. It's a gift from our Lord.

GANGSTER 2. Think of the flowers. And the animals. And the birds.

GANGSTER 1. Look at this pretty glass, does that want to die? No way.

HENRI. But you don't understand, I lost my job.

(*The last line of that section repeats itself:*)

But you don't understand, I lost my job.

But you don't understand, I lost my job.

But you don't understand, I lost my job.

(*Until* JIM *gets out of the chair:*)

JIM. How long do I wait?

JIM AS DIRECTOR. That's the thing, Jim. You don't know for how long. The killer could come through that door at any second... Can we get another camera right in Jim's face – I want to see every pore on his sweaty forehead. Stand by on set... Action.

Irina / Mark

What the fuck is that?

What you doing home so early?

Mark? Why do you have a –

Product sample. From a magazine. I told you about it – *Military Hardware*.

Sample? Since when has any magazine sent you a gun?

It's a replica.

Looks real.

/

Is it even legal to send someone a gun?

Replica. I'm doing an article on it so they sent it. Neat, huh?

It's new?

Why are you home?

Cos it doesn't look new.

Way they make them now. Shabby-chic.

Shabby-chic for guns?

What are you doing home?

How do you 'product test' a gun?

Replica.

/

/

/

I might open a bottle of wine.

Now?

/

Mark, we've got to talk, I'm worried about you –

Why are you home?

/

You're right.

Sorry?

I said you're right, Mark.

About what?

We should move back to Cardiff. Let's get in touch with the same estate agent that sold us this place. She seems trustworthy, doesn't she?

What are you –

Can't imagine this place has gone up in a few months. We'll lose a load on fees and… maybe we should rent it out.

What's going on?

You were right.

Apart from that revelation.

Mr Mazio.

Yes?

He showed me this graph and, he said this himself, I'll make a very good manager. He actually thanked me for sacking people.

You're a big success.

I haven't been able to see clearly but now –

Probably just the hours you've been working.

I resigned.

What?

I ate a pizza and I thought: If not now, when?

/

We sacked everyone with mental health. Mazio said they were affecting profit. He showed me a graph. He said 'that's not how a graph should look', it should go this way, not this way. We sacked all the people with, all the poor people with, and I said to him this is going to cause a shitstorm on Twitter but he has that covered. He tweeted how sad he was to see the pilot project end. He said the DWP were on his side, they were glad it ended cos it cost so much, that they never said how long it would last so how could anyone complain? They never even named it. They fucked them all over. Mr Mazio said my probation is over and that I'm on the staff and asked me how I'm going to celebrate – so I told him I'm celebrating by resigning.

You can't quit now.

You were right – this isn't the type of company I want to work for.

Are you mad?

I've decided to be positive about this.

No.

No, what? No to being positive?

No to moving. No to you –

What? You hate it here. You hate Wrexham.

It's grown on me.

In a few days you've gone from calling it a 'wasteland' to loving the place?

You ever feel like the path is clear?

Not really. Not recently.

My eyes have been opened, Irina. We don't have to do what we're supposed to do.

This is a good time to bring this up. This is the time I should say this.

Irina?

I know you've stopped taking your tablets, Mark. Or, at least, some of them.

I'm looking at Wrexham in a different light, Irina.

That's because you're not taking your meds. I found a blister packet. In the bin. Unblistered.

Can see the purpose of Wrexham now.

We can go back to Cardiff – you can see that nice doctor you liked, Dr Prisa –

I'm not leaving Wrexham.

Until we sell this place? I agree, actually, I've been thinking and do I really want to be a manager when I can be a managing director? SMEs are the backbone of the economy.

Sorry?

Enterprise is the key. Why not set up my own business? and I've been thinking about that man, the one I hired, then I sacked and I looked on Twitter and –

Should have seen this coming. Mile off.

What?

He doesn't fall in love – it's *her* that falls in love and then he comes to me and says 'don't kill me now'.

What the fuck are you on about?

I Hired a Contract Killer, Irina – it's all there.

/

Should have seen this coming.

/

Mark, please, let's talk about –

You don't understand.

Mark?

I'm never leaving Wrexham.

I thought when I told you about Mazio's you'd be pleased, you'd be –

This isn't a replica.

What?

Sit.

What?

Ring up Mazio and say you want your job back.

No.

Ring him –

No, Mark?

Ring –

Don't point that at me.

I can wait.

Mark?

We're staying together and we're staying in Wrexham, Irina.

Mark!

I am not leaving Wrexham!

Well, you can stay here but I'm –

This is not a replica, Irina.

Film / Jim

JIM *waits in his flat, waiting for his killer.*

A clip from I Hired a Contract Killer. *The Killer is waiting with Margret in her flat. He casually takes out his gun and screws in the silencer.*

Mark / Irina

Sometimes, Irina, I feel like I'm going down one of those ski runs they have, the black run for professionals and skiing types?, and I'm racing downhill and there's no stopping, but I know, at some point, I'm going to crash. You ever get that feeling?

No. I. Sorry, Mark. You're so ill. Put the gun down.

/

Mark?

Sometimes I just feel like there's a little man sat in the back of my head, with the controls, and I can see the inside of my skull and I'm looking at the man and he's looking out of these two eye sockets.

/

I've gone mad, Irina. It's finally happened, I've gone mad.

I'm so, so sorry.

Jim

JIM *is pacing the space.*

JIM AS DIRECTOR. You've hired a hitman, he's going to come in at any time, you're prepared for it but one thing is nagging away at you – and this is the beauty of a film where we can basically do anything with these green screens – you enter a sort of trance state and in that state you do get a visit. Yes, you sit, here, yes, maybe cross your legs, genius, and in this place where you will die you have a conversation. Of course your mother's been dead for three years but that doesn't freak you out. Got it? Your motivation? I think you want to tell your mother – and by extension the audience – how this all started. Okay. Stand by. Action.

JIM. Not long after you died, I was fine – people die, I know – I was reading a book. *Cat's Cradle* by Kurt Vonnegut. I turned a page and then my hands didn't look like my hands. They looked like a picture of my hands. I looked around the room and it wasn't a room but a film set made to look like the same room.

Mark / Irina

I'll never understand why you want to leave me for Jim, but I know why you don't want to be with me. It's because I'm empty inside, isn't it?

I'm not leaving you, Mark.

/

We can get you help. We can get out of here and get you –

Ha! That's funny. That's, your face! You really are a peach. *There's a little man sat in the back of my head.* Ha, ha, brilliant. *I know why you don't want to be with me. It's because I'm empty inside, isn't it?* Classic. Punked. Your face.

I've changed my mind. I'm leaving you. Now.

So what, you've had some trouble at work, get over it.

Why do you have to…?

Because you can't see the big picture. Never could.

The big picture is that you're a fucking replica just like that gun, Mark. You don't have any thoughts of your own. You're scared of having thoughts.

Sit down.

/

Sit the fuck down, Irina. Or I swear on the Bible, the Koran, the American Constitution that I will shoot you in the face.

/

Ring up and beg for your job back, Irina.

No.

Ring up Mr Motherfucking Mazio, Irina.

No.

/

/

Who's that?

On time. Wait there.

Who…? Mark?

/

I ordered takeaway.

What the fuck?

It's pepperoni.

You've ordered a pizza?

I'm fed up of cooking for you.

Fuck you, Mark.

(*The doorbell rings again.*

It's a pizza.)

Film / Jim

JIM AS DIRECTOR (*on screen*). Okay, Jim, we need some footage for the DVD release – extras, director's commentary, out-takes, interviews with the actors. Got it? Okay. Just say whatever comes to mind, Jim.

JIM. You know there was a part of me that thought, when I was approached to do this project, that it was part of my depersonalisation. But now I know I am in a film.

/

I like the fact that the hitman in the film is American. Sort of American. To me, he represents something I can never be. Biggest challenge? As an actor you have to try so hard not to turn things into negatives. Okay, you got enough? I'm going to take a nap in my trailer.

(JIM *gets up but the film continues* – JIM *is still speaking on screen. He is now the film.*)

ON-SCREEN JIM. How was working with the director? When she's sober, she's a delight. Only kidding!

JIM. No, no, that's the end of the scene.

ON-SCREEN JIM. Basically, in the film, a person is given a chance and doesn't take it – some people are going to say 'that's life'.

JIM. Wait, hold on – can we stop this? The scene has ended. Where's the director?

ON-SCREEN JIM. Life is a race – and we can't all win. Maybe some people are better off not taking part in the race at all?

(*Stage* JIM *tries to find the camera.*)

JIM. Let's stop this now, yes?

(*Stage* JIM *pulls the plug on the camera. The film goes off but then flickers back to life – what the fuck?*

Stage JIM *watches in horror as:*)

ON-SCREEN JIM. At the end of the day, maybe Jim – people like Jim – don't deserve a place in our society. We're better off without them. Shoot me for saying what everyone's thinking.

Irina / Mark

Shit.

What?

This is…

What? It's a Mazio's pizza, I thought it would funny to get a Mazio's –

It doesn't have anything on it.

It has pepperoni.

In a regular pattern.

Yeah?

Part of the reason we used for sacking Jim was that he was writing messages on the pizzas.

Not sure how this is relevant.

Sometimes don't you think the universe is telling you something?

What is this pizza telling you, Irina?

That I really do have to leave you.

A cheese and pepperoni is telling you that?

And a lot more besides. You going to allow that, Mark?

/

I'm asking you that because you have a gun, Mark.

Leave.

You sure?

It's only a replica.

/

/

Please don't leave.

I have to, Mark – you know that, don't you?

But you said, I remember you saying, you'll love me forever.

And I'll still love you – I'm just not sure we can be together. Okay? I mean, I'm not sure we can be together right now, it's not healthy for both of us. You understand, yes?

/

You going to be okay?

I've got friends. I've got the movie-night thing, the gang – I've actually got something to do I'm looking forward to – a bit of pro bono work. I'll be too busy to miss you. Man, I'm swamped. I won't even notice you're not here. How long won't you be here?

I'm not sure, I can go to my mum's, clear my – head.

That's good.

Yes?

It's the logical thing to do. Who can argue with that?

And you're going to be fine?

I'm restarting my medication. I'm seeing that therapist. I'll stop taking the Xanax. I'm going to get myself back on the straight and narrow.

I'm proud of you, Mark.

Thank you, Irina. I'm going to make you prouder. Everything's going to be okay.

Jim / Irina

JIM *is aware of the screen/camera – he's nervous of the scene going wrong:*

I'm not sure you're in this scene, Irina.

Do you use Twitter, Jim?

I might have to stop this and have another word with the director.

Insta?

She's probably snorting coke in the green room though.

TikTok?

Okay, I'll play along.

Facebook?

Just cos I don't use social media doesn't mean I can't function.

I had a pizza today with no message on it.

This is more improv, yes, like a *Dogville* sort of – thing?

When I was at Mazio's –

/ ?

Mr Mazio was constantly pointing out the complaints about messages and pictures on pizzas.

Exposition alert.

Jim, I've not been myself – I've been so focused on becoming 'something' that I forgot what's important to me. In fact, it's as if I've been watching myself – a version of me – in a film.

Tell me about it.

I don't like what I've seen.

/

I need a hug.

A real one?

/

(*They hug.*)

I'm sorry for the way I've treated you.

Do you realise you really are in a film?

No, Jim, I'm not. I'm responsible for my actions. I'm worried about where I'm heading and, Jim, I really need to help you.

You tried that – it led to me hiring an assassin. It goes like this: I hire a hitman, knowing that things are never going to get better and then I meet someone and – are you about to tell me you love me?

Okay, time out.

Someone said to me this will happen and I'll regret everything that –

I don't love you, Jim. Sorry.

We're a couple of actors and this is a set and this is what's supposed to happen in stories – I say this isn't going to happen and then the audience knows that *has* to happen. Only in this film I'm playing me and you're playing you.

This is not a film. This is not a set. I am not an actor.

/

But, Jim.

Yes?

I have an offer for you.

Film

Henri and Margaret in I Hired a Contract Killer *in her flat:*

MARGARET. What about now? Do you still want to die?

HENRI. No, not any more.

MARGARET. Because of me?

HENRI. Yes, that has made me change my mind.

Film / Mark / Jim

MARK *and* JIM *face each other. They are on stage and then, also, on screen.* MARK *is holding a gun.*

The dialogue comes from on stage:

Have you come here to try and call it off?

That's what happens in the film, Mark – in the film you don't kill me.

Have some pizza.

Look, Mark… is that a real gun?

Yes.

Today someone offered me a job.

Another pilot –

No, a real job.

Bad timing.

But I believe it this time. Irina said –

Irina?

Yes, she's setting up her own pizza company. Mr Mazio was only looking at the negative comments about me writing messages on pizzas but there was even more people commenting on how much they enjoy the messages. I'm trending, apparently. Irina's new company will have one employee – me – and I can take as long as I like making the pizzas – Irina says the longer I take the better. People think if they have to wait ages for something it makes it more valuable. Irina's calling it Sloooooow Pizzas – with plenty of Os – she's charging a fortune for some dough, tomato, cheese and a message from me –

You and Irina? Of course.

Yeah. What?

(ON-SCREEN MARK *points the gun at* JIM.)

You're really going to kill me, aren't you? This doesn't end like the film.

We made a promise to each other, Jim.

/

/

Okay.

Okay.

/

/

I'm ready for the end of the film.

Film

Cross-fade to a scene from I Hired a Contract Killer*:*

It plays on screen but JIM *says Henri's lines.* MARK *says the killer's lines.*

MARK. I'll be gone in a few weeks' time.

JIM. I'm sorry.

MARK. Why? It'll get me out of here.

JIM. Don't you like it here?

MARK. No. I'm a loser.

JIM. But this time you won.

MARK. That's what you think. Life is a disappointment. Goodbye.

/

(*Cross-fade on screen back to* MARK *and* JIM. MARK *draws back the hammer on the gun.*

The dialogue comes from on stage:)

/

/

What type of gun is it?

Glock 26. Gen 4. Nine mil.

You kept it. From the army?

No.

You ever apply for PIP, Mark?

No.

The forms are a nightmare. But that's just the start. The interview is... before that I attended a weekly self-help management course at the Jobcentre. The course lasted for six weeks and I had to attend or face sanctioning. But it was focusing more on people in pain, people who had bad backs and that. It was based on physical health, and I told them a number of times that this doesn't apply to me. I'm not in pain.

Not that type of pain.

Not that type of pain.

/

I came home from one session to find my mother dead. Immediately, the room turned into a film set. I watched Mum, in the chair, near the window, and I swear I saw her last breath. A close-up. A slight breath out and then... cut. I watched my arms as they strapped a set of kitchen knives to the front door, and the arms tied my torso to that same door. The little man in my head pulled a lever and made a threatening call to the police. The idea was they would burst in, the knives would kill me. I had a street full of police. Cordons. Tactical unit, the works. There was a hostage negotiator and everything.

Death by cop. Now that's American.

It was! But the negotiator fella got me talking about my mother and he asked would Mum like her home used in this way? It would be defiling her home. I watched me cry and I knew that man, the man I was looking at, hunched against a UPVC door would always be alone, would never have a sense of purpose, would always be bottom of the shit pile.

/

Is your wife out?

Yeah.

You can't do it here, can you?

No.

I'll leave, I'll go via the park, I'll find a quiet space there, you follow and –

Thank you.

Mark?

For telling me the truth.

If I can't do that now… then when?

I wasn't in the army for long. I tried but they wouldn't let me succeed. Of the two of us, you're the one who's been offered a job.

/

That means a lot, Jim.

/

Take it.

But –

The gun's only a replica. You don't think… I'm a writer, Jim.

No.

Look, let's call it quits.

Mark?

My turn to choose at the next movie club, yeah?

/

Yeah?

Yeah.

Really?

Get out of here, you big schmuck.

/

What you going to choose?

Something without subtitles.

Something American?

Fucking A.

You going to be okay?

Yes. My wife will be home in a bit. And I've got to write an article on this replica.

What will you say?

It's realistic.

You sure about this, Mark?

You know, when it comes down to it all I ever wanted to do, I think, was some good. Don't think I've had that opportunity until now.

We can talk more. Maybe after the film-club meeting – go to The Bank. I've been told I'm a good listener.

You are.

/

I'm not sure if the camera is still rolling or not.

Yeah. It is.

/

Thank you, Mark.

For what?

I believe you believe in me.

And now someone else believes in you. This Irina woman. She sounds nice.

/

We're friends, Jim. That's all we need sometimes, isn't it?

Sometimes.

/

I'll see you next week, Mark. At the film night. Can't wait to see what film you pick.

I hope Anne's prepared for an action movie.

Yeah.

Yeah.

/

And you're okay?

Why wouldn't I be?

/

(JIM *leaves the stage and the screen*.)

/

(ON-SCREEN MARK *shoots stage* MARK *in the head*.

JIM *comes back on stage, holding a camera*.)

JIM AS DIRECTOR. Just keep on doing what you're doing. I'll keep the camera rolling after this scene has ended, don't freak out! It's a director thing. This is going to look great when we add in the green-screen footage. So you just keep doing what you're doing, yeah? And hold it… and hold it… and cut!

(*Credits.*

The End.)

Theatr Clwyd

The award-winning Theatr Clwyd is Wales' biggest producing theatre. Since 1976 Theatr Clwyd has created exceptional theatre from its home in Flintshire, North Wales. Driven by the vision and dynamism of award-winning Artistic Director Tamara Harvey and Executive Director Liam Evans-Ford, Theatr Clwyd pushes theatrical boundaries creating world-class productions.

Theatr Clwyd's recent partnership with the National Theatre led to the creation of *Home, I'm Darling* which won Best New Comedy at the Olivier Awards and was nominated in five categories including Best Set Design and Best Costume Design. Other projects of note include the UK Theatre Award-winning musical *The Assassination of Katie Hopkins*, the site specific, immersive *Great Gatsby* and the Menier Chocolate Factory co-production of *Orpheus Descending*.

Theatr Clwyd is one of only four theatres in the UK to build sets and props, make costumes and paint scenery in-house. Their impressive team of workshop, wardrobe and scenic artists, props makers and technicians ensure the skills vital to a vibrant theatre industry are nurtured right in the heart of Wales, developing the theatre makers of the future. In addition to this, Theatr Clwyd hosts an artist development programme, trainee technicians' scheme and an eighteen-month traineeship for directors, to develop the Artistic Directors of the future.

Theatr Clwyd works in the community across all art forms and is recognised as a cultural leader for its cross-generational theatre groups, work in youth justice and diverse programme of arts, health and wellbeing. Award-winning Community Engagement projects include *Arts from the Armchair*, in partnership with Betsi Cadwaladr University Health Board, which uses theatrical making skills to help people with early onset memory loss and their carers, and *Justice In A Day*, working in schools and the law courts to help at risk children to realise the consequences of crime.

During the Covid-19 pandemic, the theatre has been active in helping its community, from hosting blood donation sessions and distributing food to vulnerable families, to creating digital dance workshops for those with Parkinson's and sharing creative packages and activities with those most isolated.

www.theatrclwyd.com

www.nickhernbooks.co.uk

facebook.com/nickhernbooks

twitter.com/nickhernbooks